You Can't Take it With You

Requests for information should be addressed to:
Zondervan, *Grand Rapids, Michigan 49530*

978-0-310-31848-4

Interior Design By Melissa Elenbaas

Printed In China

09 10 11 12 • 5 4 3 2 1

Content in this book excerpted from *When the Game Is Over, It All Goes Back in the Box* by John Ortberg.

Stuff, Stuff And
More Stuff

We all have stuff. We see it, want it, buy it, display it, insure it, and compare it with other people's stuff. We talk about whether or not they have too much stuff; we envy or pass judgment on other people's collections of stuff. We collect our own little pile. We imagine that if that pile got big enough, we would feel successful or secure.

That's how you keep score in Monopoly, and that's how our culture generally keeps score as well.

You get a house, then you have to get stuff to put in it. You keep getting more stuff, and you need a bigger house. A house, said comedian George Carlin, is just a pile of stuff with a cover on it. Some people have actually survived without owning one.

There are now more than 30,000 self-storage facilities in the country offering over a billion square feet for people to store their stuff. In the 1960s, this industry did not exist. We now spend $12 billion a year just to pay someone to store our extra stuff! It's larger than the music industry.

Psychologist Paul Pearsall comments on people finding it difficult to give their stuff away:

"Many people can't bring themselves to get rid of any of their stuff.

You may require a 'closet exorcist.' A trusted friend can help prevent the 'Re-stuffing phenomenon.' Re-stuff happens when, in the process of cleaning out closets and drawers, we are somehow stimulated to acquire new stuff. Beware of the stuff co-addicts, who may see a closet cleaning as a chance to acquire stuff for themselves from your stuff supply. Such friends are likely to go with you on a re-stuffing expedition."

Some people have a gift for acquiring stuff. Not long ago I took my daughter to a place called Hearst Castle. William Randolph Hearst was a "stuffaholic." He had 3,500-year-old Egyptian statues, medieval Flemish tapestries, and centuries-old hand-carved ceilings, and some of the greatest works of art of all time.

[Hearst] built a house of 72,000 square feet to put his stuff in. He acquired property for his house–265,000 acres; he originally owned fifty miles of California coastline. He collected stuff for eighty-eight years. Then you know what he did?

He died.

Now people go through Hearst's house by the thousands. They all say the same thing: "Wow, he sure had a lot of stuff."

People go through life, get stuff, and then they die, leaving all their stuff behind. What happens to it? The kids argue over it. The kids—who haven't died yet, who are really just pre-dead people—go over to their parents' house. They pick through their parents' old stuff like vultures, deciding which stuff they want to take to their houses. They say to themselves, "Now this is my stuff." then they die—and some new vultures come for it.

People come and go. Nations go to war over stuff, families are split apart because of stuff. Husbands and wives argue more about stuff than any other single issue.

YOU CAN'T TAKE IT WITH YOU

Prisons are full of street thugs and CEOs who committed crimes to acquire [stuff].

Why? It's only stuff. Houses and hotels are the crowning jewels in Monopoly. But the moment the game ends they go back in the box. So it is with all our stuff.

Christ said, "Do not store up for yourselves treasures on earth, where moth and rust destroy, and where thieves break in and steal. But store up for yourselves treasures in heaven, where moth and rust do not destroy, and where thieves do not break in and steal. For where your treasure is, there your heart will be also."

Matthew 6:20

Let's say you spend a week at Motel 6. How likely would it be for you to take all your money and spend it decorating your motel room? How probable is it that you would clean out your bank account to purchase Van Goghs or paintings of Elvis on velvet or whatever it is that your taste runs to?

Not very. You wouldn't even be tempted, because the motel room is not home. You're only going to be there a little while. It would be foolish to waste the treasure of your one and only life on a temporary residence.

[Life] is Motel 6. Your "room"—your home and furniture and clothes and possessions—will last the equivalent of a few seconds compared to the eternity that will be occupied by your soul. It's not bad to stay in a place and enjoy it while you're there. [but] ... don't store up treasure in Motel 6. It's not home. You're only going to be here a little while. If you're going to stay up nights dreaming, dream about something better than how to upgrade your motel room.

Smart players are clear on what lasts and what doesn't. So Jesus says it is wise to store up treasure in what's eternal: God and people.

To an adult, it's ironic when a two-year-old says, "Mine."

Adults know that two-year-olds don't earn any of their stuff. It is all provided for them. It is a gift from someone much larger and wiser than they. They don't even generally take very good care of it.

Nevertheless, two-year-olds get extremely attached to their stuff. If someone tries to take something, that item suddenly becomes their favorite stuff. Two-year-olds can be so deluded, can't they?

A greedy man stirs up dissention.

Proverbs 28:25

The wicked man ... blesses the greedy and reviles the LORD.

Psalm 10:3

The earth is the LORD's and everything in it, the world and all who live in it.

Psalm 24:1

Everything on earth will perish.

Genesis 6:17

Riches do not endure forever.

Proverbs 27:24

How Little Can
You Give?

I have been around churches for a long time. Do you know what the most frequently asked question about tithing is? "Do I have to tithe on the net or on the gross?" Translation: "How little can I give and not get God mad at me?" The implied question is, "How much of *my stuff* can I keep and not get in trouble?" This is like going to your mom on Mother's Day and saying, "Mom, what's the least amount of money I can spend on your present without severing our relationship?"

One day we will give an account for what God has entrusted to us. That can be an occasion of great joy or of deep regret. Some time ago we borrowed a friend's car. We had a two-car garage that was full; our friend's car was sitting in the driveway. We have five drivers in our family; three of them are teenagers. Somebody got into a car in the garage and backed out without checking the rearview mirror. *Boom!* I don't want to tell you who it was because I don't want to embarrass that person. It was not, however, one of the teenage drivers. Nor was it my wife. What a bad feeling I had when it was time to return the car: "Here's what you entrusted to me. I didn't do real well with it. I had an accident—in the driveway."

YOU CAN'T TAKE IT WITH YOU

It's not my stuff. And one day I will give
account.

One of the most amazing statements about the early church is that "There were no needy persons among them." If they had stuff, they shared it. There had never been a community like this.

A greedy man brings trouble to his family.
Proverbs 15:27

Christ said, "Be on your guard against all kinds of greed."

Luke 12:15

We Leave Naked
and Penniless

.

Speaker Randy Alcorn sometimes invites his listeners to go for an imaginary ride. We're in line behind a few dozen pickups. They are filled with old furniture and rusted refrigerators and obsolete TV sets and velvet pictures of Elvis. One by one they stop at the top of a hill; the drivers get out and throw the stuff from their trucks over the edge of the hill to whatever's below.

You get out of your car to look over the edge and see what's going on. You see nothing but acres and acres of junk. It is old stuff home. It used to be called a junkyard or a dump, but nobody wants to live next to one of those, so now we call it a "landfill."

Garbage and dump and junk are sad words, but filling up land with more land sounds positive. Who doesn't want the world to have more land?

It's a dump all the same, and that's where old stuff goes to die. Flat screen TVs and subzero refrigerators … and toasters and Twinkies and pieces of old Lear jets will rot next to each other in the democracy of decay. It's not that such treasures are bad. It's that they won't last. Stuff is a foolish investment. It's all going back in the box.

YOU CAN'T TAKE IT WITH YOU

Paul says, "People who want to get rich fall into temptation and a trap and into many foolish and harmful desires that plunge men into ruin and destruction."

1 Timothy 6:9

Not having stuff can lead you into the trap. Ironically, getting more doesn't lead to more freedom. Getting can be its own trap.

We are desiring creatures. We can't stop desiring any more than we can stop breathing.

Mail-order catalogs are in the "need-creating" business. Things that we used to put in the "want" category keep getting shifted into the "need" category, and we feel we can't get along without them. We suffer from "catalog-induced anxiety." Here's the problem: you cannot get enough of what you do not need.

We come in naked and penniless; we're going out naked and penniless. In between we get some stuff to put on our bodies and some stuff in our pockets, but none of it is really ours. We borrow it for a while; then one day we will hand it all back in.

My desire for financial security discourages me from giving. Each dollar I give away is no longer available for my protection. But my sense of freedom always *increases* when I give because giving is a declaration that my security rests someplace other than the bank. Giving is an act of confidence in God.

Jon Haidt is a University of Virginia professor who found himself worn down by the study of human pathology. He began to explore that which elevates the human spirit to try to find out what creates lasting joy. He calls such emotion "elevation."

Psychology professor, Martin Seligman, engaged his class in a debate about whether happiness comes more readily from acts of kindness or from having fun. He gave them a unique assignment: engage in one philanthropic activity and one pleasurable activity and write about both. "The results were life-changing. The afterglow of the pleasurable activity (hanging out with friends, or watching a movie or eating a hot fudge sundae) paled with the effects of the kind action. When our philanthropic acts were spontaneous and called upon personal strengths, the whole day went better."

When we give casually, we receive casual joy. When we give ... thoughtfully, creatively, we get immense joy.

In the Old Testament, David was once offered everything he needed to give an offering to God. He turned it down, saying, "Shall I give to the Lord that which costs me nothing?" David understood how satisfaction comes to the human heart.

The righteous give generously.

Psalm 37:21

Richness of Being

Yale theologian Miroslav Volf says that there are two kinds of richness in life: "Richness of having" and "richness of being." Richness of having is an external circumstance. Richness of being is an inner experience.

We usually focus on richness of having. We think true happiness lies there. Our language reflects this when the "haves" keep popping up in our thoughts:

If only I could have my dream house. . .

If only I could have a higher salary. . .

When I have a better car. . .

When I have enough money for the ultimate vacation. . .

If only I could have financial security/nicer clothes/better vacations/shinier toys. . .

We seek richness of having, but what we really want is richness of being. We want to be grateful, joyful, content, free from anxiety, and generous. We scramble after richness of having because we think it will produce richness of being, but it does not.

In the sense of "having," we can become rich by long hours, shrewd investments, and a lot of luck. But it is possible to *have* a barn full of money and a boatload of talent and movie star good looks and still *be* poor.

The bottomless pit of our desires will never be satisfied. No matter how much we have, we remain "not-enough people." For not-enough people, there exists no lasting soul satisfaction. I saw an ad this week that featured the tagline "yesterday I didn't know it existed; today I can't live without it." That is the disease of the not-enough soul.

We can have very little and yet *be* rich. A rich soul experiences life differently. It experiences a sense of *gratitude* for what it has received, rather than resentment for what it hasn't gotten. It faces the future with hope rather than anxiety.

The Apostle Paul ... experienced richness of being. He became a "more-than-enough" person. He found that whether he was living in luxury or living in prison he had more than enough, because he had been freed from the treadmill of having.

Richness of being is always available. I can seek at any time, with God's help, to be compassionate, generous, grateful, and joyful. And stuff can aid me in this. But usually it will not mean seeking to accumulate more stuff. Richness of having usually means getting more stuff; richness of being is generally associated with giving more stuff.

He who gives to the poor will lack nothing.
Proverbs 28:27

A good name is more desirable than great riches.
Proverbs 22:1

Busy, Busy, Busy

The [game] board that you and I play on comes in the shape of a calendar. It is filled with squares, and each square is another day. We live one square at a time.

Some people think they can squeeze everything into the box if they just try hard enough. They don't want to pay the price of *not* dong anything, so they just keep trying to jam more into their schedules. Sooner or later they end up with all the peace and serenity of a disgruntled postal employee.

Sometimes people try another approach. They attempt to microwave their priorities into marble-size commitments so they can squeeze them in alongside everything else. Pray on the run, skim over relationships, serve when they can, look for occasional laughs at a movie or a party. Many people aren't really living their priorities. They're just trying to do guilt management.

An old saying goes, "If the Devil cannot make you bad, he will make you busy." Either way you miss out on the life God intended for you to lead.

Trust God with your time. Trust that if God wants the lawn to get mowed and the snow to get shoveled, he will help you find a way to get it done. Maybe some things won't get done.

Be still before the LORD and wait patiently for him.
Psalm 37:7

How to Play the Game

I was a ten-year-old sitting at the Monopoly table. I had it all—money and property, houses and hotels. I had been a loser at this game my whole life, but today was different, as I knew it would be. Today I was Donald Trump, Bill Gates, Ivan the Terrible. Today my Grandmother was one roll of the dice away from ruin. And I was one roll of the dice away from the biggest lesson life has to teach; the absolute necessity of arranging our life around what matters in light of our mortality and eternity. It is a lesson that some of the smartest people in the world forget but that my Grandmother was laser clear on.

Here is the irrefutable truth about games that my Grandmother would try to teach me as she risked everything for Boardwalk while I tried to hang on to my little cache; when you start something, you never know what the outcome will be. If you play the game, you may lose. But if you never play the game, you definitely will never win.

Give thanks to the LORD, for he is good.

Psalm 106:1

Grow in Gratitude

The illusion of gratitude is that we will experience it more if we get new stuff that we really want. The reality is that making sure a child gets everything he or she wants is the surest way to dull the child's sense of gratitude.

Some researchers have concluded that grateful people experience what they call a low threshold of gratitude. That is, just as a whisper has to reach a certain decibel level before we hear it, goodness has to reach a certain experiential level before we perceive it. And just as some of us are hard of hearing, some of us are "hard of thanking." It takes a gift of epic proportions (winning the lottery or getting a new car) before we actually feel grateful. People with a high capacity for thankfulness, on the other hand, have a low threshold for gratitude. They find that a sunset or smile from a friend can set off a sense that they have been blessed by a gift they did not earn.

Mission Possible

Christ said, "You are the salt of the earth." But salt does not exist for itself. When is the last time you went to someone's home for a meal and said, "Man, this is great salt. Honey, how come we don't have salt like this at home? We gotta switch brands."

Salt's calling is to lose itself in something much bigger and more glorious; and then it fulfills its destiny. We were made to count. We were made to be salt. But the quest for significance is a delicate dance. If I do it *by* myself *for* myself, it's death. If I do it *with* God *for* others, it's life, because whatever I do with God for others does not go back in the box.

You and I were created to have a mission in life. We were made to make a difference. This is how the game is played.

But if we do not pursue the mission for which God made us, we will find a substitute. We cannot live in the absence of purpose. If we do not live our God-assigned mission, we will live what might be called a shadow mission, playing a game we were not meant to play.

In an old black-and-white movie named *Key Largo*, a rapacious gangster played by Edward G. Robinson, whose life is filled with violence and deceit, holds a family hostage. Someone asks him what drives him to lead this kind of life—what he wants. His face clouds over; he is not a reflective man and doesn't know how to answer the question. One of the hostages, played by Humphrey Bogart, suggests an answer: "I know what you want. You want more."

Robinson's face brightens. "Yeah, that's it. That's what I want. I want *more*." His character believes the myth of more, the myth that one day more will be enough. If we believe this myth, we spend our lives looking for the next thing. It might be a car, or a promotion, or the love of a beautiful woman. It might be, depending on our age, an iPod, or a Lamborghini, or Tickle Me Elmo.

We keep hoping that the next thing will be it—the source of true satisfaction for our souls. For a few minutes, or perhaps days, we experience true soul satisfaction. Then it wears off. It always wears off. But we always want more of the board and to be its master.

God satisfies the thirsty and fills the hungry with good things.

Psalm 107:9

Who's Materialistic?
Not Me!

We are all against materialism. In a recent extensive survey, 89 percent of the Americans who were polled said the United States is too materialistic. By sheer coincidence, almost exactly the same percentage of us said we wanted even more for ourselves. We don't want to be materialistic! We just want more.

When we try to be happy by getting more, we live on what is sometimes called the "hedonic treadmill." This means we rapidly adapt to and take for granted acquisitions and achievements in our life. When we acquire what we want, we feel a little thrill of gratification. Before we get it, we feel a lack. We think that the acquisition will make that sense of lack go away, but like Lassie, dissatisfaction always comes back home. The only "more" we end up receiving is more wanting.

The condition underneath all my wanting is that what I really want is God, and for creation to be set right by God, beginning with that little piece of creation that is my body and soul.

Do we Want the
Journey or the
Destination?

We see ourselves on a long journey that crosses mountains and plains. We are on a train, and out the window is an endless procession of cars motoring down nearby highways, children waving up at us from crossings, cows grazing on distant hillsides, fields of corn and wheat curtseying in the breeze, lakes and rivers, city skylines, and village halls.

But we don't really notice. What we keep thinking about is the final destination.

We will arrive at the station to marching bands and waving flags. Once we get there, our dreams will be fulfilled. The jigsaw pieces of our lives will finally be assembled, the picture will finally be complete. In the meantime, we restlessly roam the aisles, checking our watches, ticking off the stops; always waiting, waiting, waiting for the station.. Always wishing the train would go faster.

The name of the train is *more*. The name of the station is *satisfaction*.

"When we reach the station, that will be it!" We cry.

"When I'm eighteen."

"When I buy a new 450SL Mercedes."

"When I get the next promotion."

"When I lose enough weight."

"When we get married and have kids in the house."

"When I have paid off the mortgage."

"When we finally retire and all the pressure is off, then I will live happily ever after."

We keep thinking that train called *more* will get us to a station called *satisfaction*.

What if trying to pursue satisfaction by having more is like trying to run after the horizon? Why would we ever expect more to be enough here if this is not our home?

What if the train is called *contentment*? What if the station is called *Heaven*?

What if the station is real and is to be the object of our truest and deepest longings? Then we will see God face-to-face. Then our longings for glory, beauty, love, and meaning will be fully realized. Then the restless human race will finally cry out, "Enough!"

And God will say, "More!"

Of course, we all say that relationships are more important than money. But we constantly cheat relationships for the sake of work or money. There are no TV shows called "Who Wants To Be A Great Friend?" What we have come to call "reality" shows are programs that deliberately pit one person against another.

"Reality" means having someone excluded or fired or voted off the show. If we're going to play the game wisely, there are a few relational realities we need to observe.

Become the kind of player other people want to sit next to. The Bible's word for this is grace. Play with grace. Cultivate a gracious spirit.

Winning Gracefully

When we played games with my Grandmother, she was always fun, but she was also on the lookout for grandchildren who would sulk or pout when they lost (generally that was me, although I had a cousin with the same disease). She would always beat them (generally me). I did not like this quality in her at the time, but I understand it better now. My Grandmother was trying to teach me about one of the great challenges of life. In the short run, it seems as though you can build up self-esteem in a child by letting the child win. But in the long run, true esteem comes only from knowing we can actually handle reality, which means both wins and losses.

In an era of flamboyant end-zone celebrations and grandiose trash talking, winning gracefully is perhaps harder than loving gracefully. When I win, I'm tempted by arrogance, power, insensitivity, gloating, and wanting to relive my successes long after everyone else is bored by them. Graceful winners always remember what it feels like to lose. And they are caught up in something bigger than their own wins and losses.

When you play the game, you may win or you may lose, but for certain you will be wounded. And to deal with that hurt, you need that greatest kind of grace available: the grace to forgive.

Too much of my life has been about collecting trophies. Living for trophies leaves me hollow, empty, depressed, and tired. Trophies bring a momentary pleasure that can be addicting, but the pleasure always wears off. This is why in heaven when images like "crowns" are used, people are constantly casting them at the Lord's feet. When you give glory and praise and honor away, they bring joy; when you hoard them, they tarnish and fade and become a burden.

When we try to impress people we think are important, we're trophy collectors. "I am making a deeper impression on the cosmos because I know this famous person. When the ark sails I will be on it." All sorts of objects can become trophies: our grades, our houses, people we have impressed, our bodies, promotions, compliments, clothing labels. There are now websites where you can go to look for trophy wives—women whose beauty is a tribute to their husbands' wealth and power. A trophy is anything you can get other people to look at that will make them say, "Wow."

My Grandmother guarded her heart. [playing Monopoly] She didn't collect many houses or hotels, but that's not why she was going around the board. She honored what mattered most. She left a legacy of life and faith and love that lives on in my brother and sister and me, and in those we love. She always understood one simple truth that a lot of really smart people seem to have trouble remembering: it all goes back in the box.

In the Middle Ages the main lesson of this book was taught using the game of chess. "When the board is put away the game is ended, and the men are all put into a bag, and the king lies as often at the bottom as at the top, wherefore the men are then all alike. When time is put away by death, the game is at an end. . .all are equal in the bag of the earth."

Bishop Kenneth Ulmer is the pastor of a church that meets in Los Angeles at the forum where the Lakers used to play basketball. He tells the story of two men in a museum who see a painting of a chess game. One character in the painting looked like a man; the other looked very much like the Devil. The man was down to his last piece. The title of the painting was Checkmate.

One of the two men looking at the painting was an international chess champion. Something about the painting intrigued him. "It's titled *Checkmate*," he said, "but the title is wrong. *The king still has one more move.*"

A little boy named David is up against a giant named Goliath. David is so small he can't even wear grown-up armor or hold a grown-up sword. It looks like checkmate. *But the king still has one more move.*

A man named Daniel is thrown into a den of lions because he refuses to stop praying to his God. The lions are hungry, and he's in there all night. At the first light of dawn, King Darius calls down. Daniel tells him the lions have been put on a low-protein diet and he's doing fine. *The king still has one more move.*

A man named Moses convinces a nation of oppressed slaves to run away from the most powerful man on earth. Pharoah sets out after them. They're standing on the shore, the Red Sea in front of them, the greatest army in the world behind them. The people say to Moses, "What were you thinking?" *But the king still has one more move.*

One day it's all going back in the box. You may have thought in this life that you were master of the board. Or you may have played the role of a pawn. Stuff and titles and what passes for good fortune this time around the game board don't really amount to all that much.

Don't Despair. Live
wisely. The King Still
Has One More Move.

Text in this title was excerpted from *When the Game Is Over it All Goes Back in the Box* by John Ortberg. This title is available at your local bookstore.

978-0-310-25350-1